... because we are all holding each other
through a dance of joy and love.

This is a book about hugging.

Hugging is an instinct, a natural response to feelings of affection, compassion, need, and joy.

Hugging is also a science, a simple method of support, healing, and growth, with measurable and remarkable results.

In its highest form, hugging is also an art.

Techniques of hugging are described here with a cheerful mix of whimsy and seriousness. May they serve as a framework for you to create your own experience and practice as a Hug Therapist.

HUG THERAPY

(Kathleen Keating)

Drawings by Mimi Noland

MJF BOOKS

NEW YORK

This edition published by MJF Books
Fine Communications
Two Lincoln Square
60 West 66th Street
New York, NY 10023

Library of Congress Catalog Card Number 94-74192
ISBN 1-56731-068-0

I embrace with honor

My daughter, Ann Maureen Keating,
and all those at her special place of learning
for the developmentally disabled,
St. Vincent School in Santa Barbara, California

and my son, Matthew Roy Keating

I embrace with gratitude

Golda Clendenin, who inspired me

My friends and colleagues at Woodview-Calabasas
Hospital, who supported me

Esalen Institute for teaching me

David Gorton for believing in me

hug (hug) v.t. hugged, hugging, hugs.

> 1. to clasp or hold closely, especially in one's arms; embrace or enfold, as in affection
> 2. to cherish, hold fast
> 3. to keep very close to

hug n.

> An affectionate embrace. (From Scandinavian, akin to old Norse *hugga*, to comfort, console.)

hug therapy

> The practice of administering hugs for the purpose of curing or healing, or of preserving health. Treatment of dis-ease through the simple, physical means of hugging.

THE
HUG THERAPY
BOOK

About hugging and huggers

A hug makes you feel good all day.

Theory

Touch is not only nice. It's needed. Scientific research supports the theory that stimulation by touch is absolutely necessary for our physical as well as our emotional well-being.

Therapeutic touch, recognized as an essential tool for healing, is now part of nurses' training in several large medical centers. Touch is used to help relieve pain and depression and anxiety, to bolster patients' will to live, to help premature babies—who have been deprived of touch in their incubators—grow and thrive.

Various experiments have shown that touch can:

> Make us feel better about ourselves and our surroundings;

> Have a positive effect on children's language development and IQ;

> Cause measurable physiological changes in the toucher and the touched.

We are just beginning to understand the power of touch.

While there are many forms of touching, we propose that hugging is a very special one that contributes in a major way to healing and health.

Rationale

HUGGING

Feels good

Dispels loneliness

Overcomes fears

Opens doors to feelings

Builds self-esteem ("Wow! *She* actually wants to hug *me!*")

Fosters altruism ("I can't believe it, but I actually *want* to hug that old son-of-a-gun!")

Slows down aging; huggers stay younger longer

Helps curb appetite; we eat less when we are nourished by hugs—and when our arms are busy wrapped around others

HUGGING ALSO

Eases tension

Fights insomnia

Keeps arm and shoulder muscles in condition

Provides stretching exercise if you are short

Provides stooping exercise if you are tall

Offers a wholesome alternative to promiscuity

Offers a healthy, safe alternative to alcohol and other drug abuse *(better hugs than drugs!)*

Affirms physical being

Is democratic; anyone is eligible for a hug

HUGGING ALSO

Is ecologically sound, does not upset the environment

Is energy-efficient, saves heat

Is portable

Requires no special equipment

Demands no special setting; anyplace from a doorstep to an executive conference room, from a church parlor to a football field, is a fine place for a hug!

Makes happy days happier

Makes impossible days possible

Imparts feelings of belonging

Fills up empty places in our lives

Keeps on working to dispense benefits even after the hug's release

Besides, hugging prevents war.

ualifications

The qualifications for being a Hug Therapist and being a client are the same: just being.

Therapeutic hugging is a mutually healing process. In fact, hugger and hugged play interchangeable roles. As a Hug Therapist, you are open to the child within you who needs love, safety, support, caring, and play, and you are reaching out to the same needs in the other.

A Hug Therapist does not blame or judge. But he or she does recognize that many of us, in our standoffish society, have not learned to ask for the emotional support we need. If love or support—or play—has been skimpy since childhood, we may feel wounded. If the twistings of growing up have left us with low self-esteem, we may feel unlovable—unhuggable.

Hug Therapists can't solve all these problems, but they can respect the struggles and offer understanding, laughter, gentle words, and an abundance of hugs.

Hug Therapy is not just for the lonely or hurting ones. Hug Therapy can make the healthy healthier, the happy happier, and the most secure among us feel even more so.

Hugging is for everybody.

Anyone can be a Hug Therapist. But if you master the Types of Hugs and the Advanced Techniques presented in this book, you will develop further skills and confidence in your natural ability to share wonderful hugs.

Ethics and rules of conduct

When you are a truly professional Hug Therapist, you take full responsibility for what you say or do. Therefore the hugs you share must be thoughtful, respectful, and care-filled.

These are understood rules of conduct for Hug Therapists:

1. *Since Hug Therapy is always nonsexual, hug accordingly.* Be sure that the hugs you dispense are compassionate, not passionate. A caring, comforting, or playful hug is different from a lover's embrace. We usually recognize the difference.

No.

If you started out offering or wanting a supportive hug, and it has taken on overtones of greater physical intimacy, just recenter your feelings and thoughts on the original purpose of the hug — to give mutual support.

If you are clear about the kind of hug you are giving, the other hugger most likely will respond in kind. If not, you may want to have a talk about the importance of just-friendly hugs in your relationship.

Yes.

2. *Be certain you have permission before giving a hug.* Often permission to hug is implicit in a relationship. Your sweetheart or a close friend probably will welcome hugs almost any time. However you still need to respect the other's need for privacy and space.

Sometimes you will receive nonverbal permission from someone who wants a hug, and you respond spontaneously. Or pave the way to hugging with a simple comment like, "I would like to give you a hug." Respect the other's verbal and nonverbal messages. Most of the time you will be aware of what is needed and acceptable.

If you misread someone who did not find a hug comfortable, don't be concerned. For some, hugging is very hard; sometimes a sturdy trust must be built before they feel safe enough to hug. Although we Hug Therapists believe the gift of touch to be extremely important, the gift of acceptance is just as important!

Ask first.

3. *Also be sure to ask permission when <u>you</u> need a hug.* Hug Therapists are not only dispensers of hugs but recipients too. Huggers must sometimes be huggees. Hugging-for-health is a practice of sharing, rather than of just giving or just taking.

When you feel the need for a hug, say: "I would like a hug, if it's all right with you." Or, "I could really use a huge hug right now — would you oblige?" Or, "How about a hug before I go off to work (or to a meeting or a match or an interview or whatever). A post-hug "thank you" or "that felt good" is an important validation of the other's support.

May I have this hug?

4. *Be responsible for expressing what you need and the way you want it.* Blaming others because we're not getting what we need from them is a common mistake we make in our relationships. Some are naturally fine-tuned and intuitive about others' needs and comforts. But most of us—especially if we are busy worrying about our own insecurities—need direct, explicit communication.

If we want more hugs, fewer hugs, ten-second hugs, or two-minute-over-easy hugs—any kind of hug that may be different from what we're getting—we need to say so. Then we have to be willing to compromise as well as to realize that we won't always get exactly what we want when we want it.

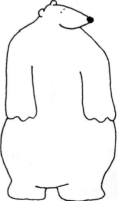

For some, hugging is very hard.

Contraindications

A MYTH AND A MODEL

While Hug Therapists are convinced that hugging is for everyone, a few doubters have trouble accepting Hug Therapy. They believe, erroneously, that the sole purpose of a hug is to build a relationship of physical intimacy.

A physically intimate embrace can be beautiful too, but it meets a different level of need. This kind of embrace will never replace a good old therapeutic hug! Even intimate partners need bundles of ordinary hugs too.

To keep little ones from acquiring this narrow view of hugs, hug them often — affectionately, supportively, playfully, and tenderly. Let them see parents and other adults hugging in these ways. Otherwise they may grow up believing that hugs are for lovers only, and that in order to be hugged — and huggable — one must be physically attracted to the other hugger.

A Hug Therapist makes every effort to share the broader understanding of touch and hugging and the faith that a day filled with hugs can bring untold satisfaction and serenity.

Fees

Hug Therapy is not free. The cost is the strength it requires to be vulnerable. The fee for hugging is the risk that our hugs will be rebuffed or misinterpreted.

When we are very young we are naturally open. We want to give love and touch as much as we want to get love and be touched. If we're deprived of love and touch, we become unwilling to pay the fee of vulnerability. Love held back can turn to pain.

Hug therapists can help ease this pain. When we risk our hugs, we affirm our wonderful ability to share. As we reach out and touch others, we are free to discover the compassion—along with the capacity for joy—that exists in all of us. As we become more spontaneous huggers and find such inner riches, the fees seem relatively small.

Thank goodness we have our softer sides.

Types of hugs

Bear hug

In the traditional bear hug (named for members of the family Ursidae, who do it best), one hugger usually is taller and broader than the other, but this is not necessary to sustain the emotional quality of bear-hugging. The taller hugger may stand straight or slightly curved over the shorter one, arms wrapped firmly around the other's shoulders. The shorter of the pair stands straight with head against the taller hugger's shoulder or chest, arms wrapped—also firmly!—around whatever area between waist and chest that they will reach. Bodies are touching in a powerful, strong squeeze that can last five to ten seconds or more.

We suggest you use skill and forbearance in making the hug firm rather than breathless. Always be considerate of your partner, no matter what style of hug you are sharing.

The feeling during a bear hug is warm, supportive, and secure.

Bear hugs are for:

Those who share a common feeling or a common cause.

Parents and offspring. Both need lots of reassuring bear hugs.

Grandparents and grandoffspring. Don't leave grandparents out of family bear hugs.

Friends (this includes marrieds and lovers, who hopefully are friends too).

Anyone who wants to say, wordlessly, "You're terrific!" Or, "I'm your friend; you can count on me." Or, "I share whatever pain or joy you're feeling."

What can a bear hug say for you?

The A-frame hug

Stand facing each other, wrapping arms around shoulders, sides of heads pressed together and bodies leaning forward and not touching at all below shoulder level. There. You have an A-frame hug. The length of time spent in the A formation is usually brief, since this is often a "hello" or "goodbye" hug.

The underlying feeling may be one of polite caring or detached warmth.

The A-frame hug is most appropriate for new acquaintances or professional colleagues, or in situations that require a degree of formality. Because it is relatively nonthreatening, it is comfortable for shy or unpracticed huggers.

This is a classic hug and should not be discounted because of its formal quality. It has broad application and is therefore beneficial to a wide range of huggers.

An A-frame hug is particularly apt for:

A great-aunt whom you haven't seen since you were a toddler.

Your spouse's employer's husband.

Your former academic adviser.

A new daughter-in-law.

Who else?

Like this.

Cheek hug

The cheek hug is a very tender, gentle hug that often has a spiritual quality. It can be experienced comfortably sitting down, standing up, or even with one sitting and one standing, as full body contact is not necessary.

If you are both seated, turn comfortably toward each other and press the sides of your faces together cheek to cheek. One hand may be on the other's back and the other supporting the back of the head to counteract the pressure of your cheek. Breathe slowly and deeply. Within a few seconds you will feel very relaxed. The cheek hug often stirs deep feelings of kindness, especially when participants are close friends.

A cheek hug is a tasteful way to:

Greet an elderly friend or relative who is seated.

Say a wordless "I'm sorry" about a friend's disappointment.

Share a friend's joy at a happy occasion, like a wedding or graduation. (This is a considerate hug for congratulating the principals in reception lines, since it does not tangle wedding veils or crush boutonnières.)

At what times would you proffer a cheek hug?

It often has a spiritual quality.

Sandwich hug

The sandwich hug is a lesser known variety, but once you experience its warmth and security, you'll want to share this one often.

This is a hug for three. Two face each other with the third in the middle facing either one of the others. Each of the two on the outside reaches toward the waist area of the other and hugs. The one in the center wraps arms around the waist of the facing hugger. As an option, the outside pair may hug around the shoulders and all three snuggle heads together. The bodies are touching cozily.

The sandwich hug gives the one in the middle an especially secure feeling, which is helpful if she or he is going through a difficult time and needs extra support.

The sandwich hug is handy for:

Three good friends.

A couple wishing to comfort someone.

Two parents and a child. The child may be very young, grown up, or any place between.

Make your own sandwich.

Grabber-squeezer hug

The grabber-squeezer hug holds the record for brevity. One hugger runs up to and throws arms about another, gives a fast squeeze before letting go, then dashes off. The one so hugged must be alert in giving a squeeze in return, in order to receive maximum benefit from this hug.

In a variation of the grabber-squeezer, choreographically more difficult, both run toward each other and give a quick, simultaneous squeeze. Safety note: Avoid a collision course. The full-force crash of two bodies who have hurtled together or the knocking of two heads may negate some of the good feelings!

Feelings vary with the situation, but often the grabber-squeezer is accompanied by a sense of affectionate

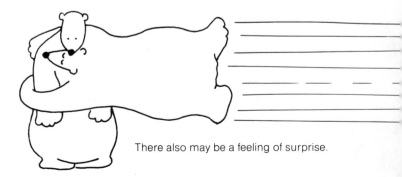

There also may be a feeling of surprise.

distraction because one or both of the huggers are rushed. If the huggee is not expecting it, there also may be a feeling of surprise.

Grab-and-squeeze hugging is a practical way to work in a lot of fast hugging when you're on a tight schedule. For more effective stress management, also include a liberal sprinkling of hugs that are gentler and last longer.

Use the grabber-squeezer:

In the workshop or the kitchen.

To wish someone luck before a performance.

As a silent translation of the words "I like you a lot, but I'm in a terrible hurry!"

How can the grabber-squeezer fit into your life?

Group hug

The group hug is a very popular hug for good friends sharing in an activity or project. As Hug Therapists, we would like the group hug to be better known and more often applied, just because it feels so good.

The group forms a circle—its members standing as close together as possible, arms around shoulders or waists—and squeezes. In a variation, group hug participants, holding each other as above, move in toward the center, shrinking the circle. They huddle together for several moments, then back up and break apart with a cheer or sigh or a quick, parting squeeze.

Besides good feelings of support, security, and affection, group hugs often impart a sense of unity and universal belonging.

Group hugs are good for:

Growth groups.

Support groups.

Classmates, teammates.

Hardworking committees.

Any bunch you like.

When would your group welcome a hug like this?

A group hug often imparts a sense of universal belonging.

Side-to-side hug

The side-to-side hug, or the lateral squeeze, is a great hug to get and give while walking along together. As you stroll side by side with an arm around the other's waist or over the shoulder, once in a while give a generous squeeze.

This is also a merry and playful hug for those moments when you are standing in line with a friend. It makes queuing up a pleasure!

The side-to-side hug provides a joyful moment while:

Walking to a bus.

On a hike or an archaeological dig.

Waiting to get into a Saturday night movie or to register for next term's classes.

When could you use a side-to-side hug?

Back-to-front hug

In the back-to-front hug (also known as the waist-grabber), the hugger approaches the other from the back, folds arms around his or her waist and gives a gentle hug.

The back-to-front waist-grabber is the perfect hug to give someone who is peeling potatoes, scrubbing pans over a kitchen sink, or otherwise engaged in some routine stand-up chore. A somewhat old-fashioned hug, this was practiced more extensively before the invention of the automatic dishwasher. But most of the time a waist-grabber is still welcome as a brief, playful gesture. The feeling behind it is happy and supportive.*

*Even more supportive would be the back-to-front hug *followed by* the picking up of a dishtowel and applying it to the pans.

Back-to-front hugs are for:

Househusbands, housewives, and other live-ins.

Co-workers on an assembly line.

Friends whose occupations require that they face mostly in one direction—like raspberry-pickers or mail-sorters.

Do you know someone who would appreciate a waist-grabber?

Heart-centered hug

Many consider the heart-centered hug to be the highest form of hugging, and official Hug Therapists feel, too, that it is indeed very powerful.

The heart-centered hug begins with direct eye contact as the two huggers stand facing each other. Then the arms are wrapped around shoulders or back. Heads are together, and there is full body contact. The hug is firm, yet gentle. As the two breathe slowly and easily together, they focus on the compassion that is flowing from one heart into the other.

There is no time limit on this hug; it may last several moments, shutting out all nearby distractions. The heart-centered hug is full and lingering, caring and tender, open and genuine, supportive and strong.

The heart-centered hug acknowledges that place at the center of each of us where—if we're open to it—pure, unconditional love may be found.

The heart-centered hug feels right:

> When the huggers are very old friends with a long history of crisscrossing paths.

> When the huggers are very new friends brought together by a shared experience and a strong, shared emotion.

When might you share a heart-centered hug?

It may last several moments, shutting out all distractions.

Custom-tailored hug

The most effective hug for you is the hug that feels right, considering the setting, the situation, the one you are with, and what you personally need from the hug (affection, strength and support, reaffirmation of a bond of friendship, relaxation, or any other good feeling that a hug can bring.)

Sometimes a custom-tailored hug is called for, as in the case of an extra-tall hugger and a very short huggee (or vice versa). Or when the hug, in order to please both parties equally, has to include a jealous pet or a favorite toy too.

Be creative. True Hug Therapists do not let circumstances stand in their way.

A custom-tailored hug may have to include a favorite toy.

Hugs: where, when, why

Environments

A place of beauty enhances the experience of hugging. Whatever setting you consider beautiful—a peaceful country path on a warm, clear day or a scrap of green park that opens a city to the sky—can make the hug you share with a friend even more special.

However, if the setting seems shabby or bleak, it can be totally transformed just because you are sharing a hug.

Anyplace is the right place for hugging when the heart is open.

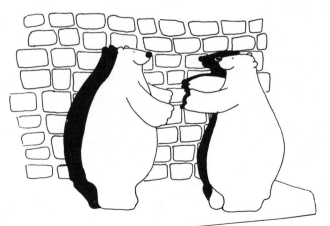

A hug transforms a bleak setting...

. . . into a lovely place.

Time of day

Some are morning, up-and-at-'em huggers. Some are evening, thank-heaven-the-day-is-over huggers. Some like to hug at high noon on lunch hours or at teatime. Although routine hugs are fine, sometimes the most appreciated hugs happen spontaneously at unexpected moments.

The feelings that bring on a hug—affection, sympathy, caring, just plain joy—can happen at any time of day. So can hug situations, like bumping into an old school friend at an airport. True Hug Therapists will entertain the idea of a hug at any time. And hugs scattered through the day will help to maintain a sense of well-being, belonging, and self-esteem.

Friendship

Compassion

Joy

Feelings that bring on a hug . . .

. . . can happen any time.

Sound effects

A hug may be accompanied by a moment of stillness.
Or it may include expressions of pleasure, like these:

(Sigh)

Whoopee!

That's nice.

Thank you. I needed that.

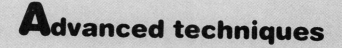

Advanced techniques

Visualization

Visualization is a powerful technique for learning and change. One way we learn is through repeated imprintings on our minds—not only of what we actually view in the world around us, but also of pictures we see in our imaginations. Imagined pictures, which can affect us as strongly as reality, sometimes even set off physical responses.

Think about slicing a juicy lemon and squeezing the tart juice into your mouth. Your mouth waters at the very thought. You may detect a sour taste, too. You have the sensation of sucking a lemon even though there's no real lemon anywhere in sight.

Now try visualizing yourself hugging somebody. Let this imagined hug register in your mind as a nourishing experience. A mind picture like this can teach you to see yourself as someone who is at ease giving and getting warm, caring hugs.

In guided imagery, you plan or guide the direction you'd like your imagination to take. So let's say you would like to be comfortable greeting a friend with a heart-centered hug. Sit in a comfortable, quiet place and close your eyes. Breathe slowly and deeply four or five times and let your body relax totally. Imagine yourself walking along and meeting a good friend. Picture the two of you saying hello by putting your arms around each other and sharing a heart-centered hug.

Keep the picture in your mind as you sense good feelings of affection and warmth. It is important to put the imagined picture and the feelings together.

Or use guided imagery when you are feeling the need for support after a stressful day. Visualize a favorite friend who is also a good hugger giving you a very fond and supportive hug. Imagine that friend holding you and offering you reassurance and love. Keep the picture and the feelings in your mind for as long as you need comfort.

An imagined hug is a nourishing experience.

Zen hugging

You can use any type of hug for Zen hugging. Our favorites are the cheek-to-cheek hug or the heart-centered hug. A very connected touch—a feet-to-feet and hands-to-hands touch, for instance—will do fine, too.

Your eyes may be open or closed. Focus on your breathing, and allow it to become even and deep. You will begin to feel yourself relaxing. You are centered in the present moment. Let go of all thinking. All that is present is the experience of your senses.

You are aware of the warmth you are sharing, of your breath moving in and out, of the touch of the other person, of the air on your skin. Relax. Be suspended in time. The longer you are able to relax in the present moment, the deeper will be your experience of the hug or the touching.

Peace.

You are centered in the present moment.

That extra touch

Hugging is just one kind of therapeutic touching. There are others too, as touch research has confirmed.

You may want to combine hugging with another nourishing kind of platonic touching, such as gentle stroking or patting.

There are other kinds of therapeutic touching too.

Hug often. Hug well.

HUG THERAPY 2

Edited by Jane Thomas Noland

. . . because we are all holding each other
through a dance of joy and love.

We have learned to speak to each other in many ways—with words, gestures, actions, postures, looks—and touch.

The *Hug Therapy Book* shows how one form of touching—the giving and receiving of warm, supportive hugs—promotes health and well-being. In *Hug Therapy 2,* discover a new dimension of hug therapy: hugs have their own special language.

May this book serve as an inspiration for you to create your own language of hugs.*

*In this book, the language of hugs—what hugs can say when they are translated into words—is always printed in *italic*.

I embrace with honor
  my father and mother, Roy and Minnie Armistead
  my sister, Christine Ann Armistead

I embrace with gratitude
  Helen Colton, for inspiring me

  My friends Lynne and Maureen De Boer, Margie
  Rinehart, Wendy McCarty Wong, Anita Liggett,
  Francie White, Cathy Davis, Judith Harkins, Sue Von
  Baeyer, Christina Essmana for supporting me

  Fred Schloessinger, for holding me with love.

Hugs speak a universal language .

communicate v.t.
1. To impart, pass along
2. To give or exchange information, thoughts, signals, or messages
3. To be connected

hug v.t.
1. To clasp or hold closely, especially in one's arms; embrace or enfold, as in affection
2. To cherish, hold fast
3. To keep very close

hug n.
An affectionate embrace (from Scandinavian, akin to old Norse *hugga,* to comfort, console)

hug therapy n.
1. The practice of administering hugs for the purpose of curing or healing, or of preserving health
2. Treatment of dis-ease through the simple, physical means of hugging

About speaking with hugs

Sorry

Thanks

Hello

Au Revoir

Peace

Whoopee

heory

Science and instinct tell us that one good way to reach the sensitive living spirit is through physical touch. And one of the most important forms of touch is a hug. With a hug, we communicate as individuals on the deepest level. With a hug, we embrace the whole of life.

We all have an inner yearning that calls us to respond with a quality of contact that affirms our potential as growing individuals. The language of hugs nourishes the spirit.

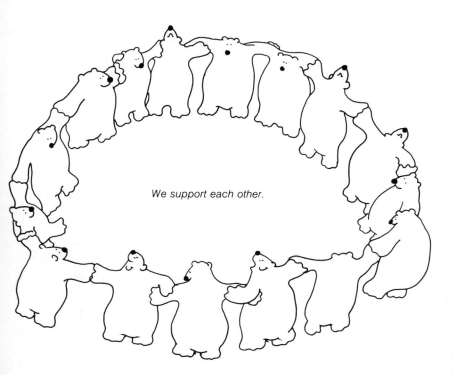

We support each other.

An embrace creates a circle of compassion that promotes growth and healing and feeds our empty hearts.

Rationale

Because we move about in a world of many languages, only the nonverbal language of touching and hugs knows no limits.

Because we live in an age of reason and technology, we are losing awareness of our senses. When we touch and hold each other in a spirit of compassion, we bring life to our senses and reaffirm our trust in our own feelings.

When technology builds barriers...

a hug tears them down.

Application

Say it with hugs to emphasize the message.

We may say aloud, "Let me know if there's any way I can help." A hug adds, *I really mean that!*

We may say aloud, "I like you." A hug adds, *I care deeply about you. In fact, I love you a lot.*

Punctuate with a hug!

Say it with hugs when words are awkward or hard to say.

We may know the appropriate words but find them really difficult to say out loud, especially if we're shy or overwhelmed by feelings. At such times we count on the language of hugs.

A hug can say things like:

I am here for you any time.

I really understand your feelings.

Please celebrate my joy with me.

Allow me to share in your sadness.

Even ordinary words like hello and goodbye are sometimes very hard to say.

Please let me help you bear this frightening time.

Say it with hugs when words can't express it.

Although we may speak from our most authentic selves as we reach into our deepest feelings, talk can only go so far. An embrace from the heart often cannot be translated into words.

When we allow ourselves to be in a still place of inner awareness, the message of vitality, spirit, and love that we all carry within us is often felt, given, and received in a place beyond language. To reduce this experience to words, either inwardly or out loud, may diminish a very profound message.

Besides using the magnificent gift of language, we must also respect intuitive, wordless wisdom and listen with our hearts. That is how we hear the greater meaning of the mystery we have named love.

Hugs have their own language.

Qualifications

Anyone can be a hug therapist. Since hug therapy is a helping technique that benefits both therapists and clients, the qualifications for being a hug therapist and being a client are the same: just being. Hugging for health is a mutually healing process for all participants.

But as a hug therapist, you take responsibility to communicate a genuine feeling of care and compassion.

Any qualified hug therapist can further develop skill and confidence by learning the special language of hugs.

Ethics

A healing hug never gives a mixed message. Instead,
a hug always speaks authentically about who we are
and what we feel; we need first to be in touch with
ourselves before we can reach out to touch someone
else. We are uncomfortable and confused when words
say one thing and an embrace says another.

I feel just wonderful. Everything is A-okay.

I'm really very sad.

A hug never says *I blame you* or *I want to cause harm.*

We are all complex individuals trying to find fulfillment. We do not have a choice about how we feel, but we can choose what we say or do in response to feelings.

We can discover ways to meet our needs without blaming or harming ourselves or others. As hug therapists, our responsibility is to create and heal, not to harm or blame. We can no longer afford to view the world in terms of "good guys" and "bad guys."

A therapeutic hug is always nonsexual.

A caring, supportive, or playful hug is different from a lover's embrace and does not invite the level of physical intimacy that is part of a romantic relationship.

I want to be your lover, baby.

I want to be your friend.

No.

Yes.

Fee

Therapeutic touching is a new language that we are just learning. The price we pay in reaching out is that others may misinterpret our hugs as intrusive or conducive to a romantic relationship.

As we become more aware of what the language of touch can say to us about affirmation and support, we will discover that hugging is healthy communication that enriches our lives. As hugging becomes more acceptable as our "second language," the fees for risking will lessen accordingly.

We are willing to risk a hug because the rewards are great.

Basics of hug language

Besides its particular message, a hug to be truly therapeutic always makes these nonverbal statements.

A therapeutic hug always says:

I understand how you feel.

Because we feel the same kinds of feelings, there is a bond of commonality that embraces us and creates unity. We respect our own feelings as a natural guidance system for making decisions, creating values, and working through problems. We validate each other's feelings as an essential part of being.

Your loss is my loss.

That's too bad.

A therapeutic hug always says:

I respect your unique inner wisdom. You are special.

We celebrate the fact that within the circle of unity are individuals whose rich diversity makes life exciting. Others' feelings, ideas, and values expand our reality beyond our limited and personal views. The world is full of endless possibilities because we are different.

A therapeutic hug always says:

You are who you are, not just what you do.

We all need the confirmation of ourselves as whole and unique beings separate from the many functional roles we must play.

Example: *You are not*  *only a doctor and a mother as well as a pitcher in a softball league and a veterinary assistant and an aerobics expert and an arbiter of disputes and a lover and a bus driver and a domestic genius—you are YOU.*

Have a hug, Clement.

A review of the most often used hugs is helpful in order to choose just the right hug to convey the message. Each hug which follows has many verbal and nonverbal translations depending on the huggers and the situation; just a few are offered here.

A dictionary of hugs

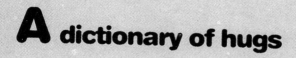

A-frame hug

Classic. Somewhat formal. Beneficial to a wide range of huggers—from brides to board members, from graduating seniors to golden-age seniors.

An A-frame hug can say:

I'd like to know you better.

Happy special occasion (whatever it may be)!

I know that you are dressed up for this festive event and would appreciate a hug that doesn't crush or wrinkle.

Ankle hug

Firm encirclement of another's ankle, usually by a hugger of small stature. Requires an immediate response, such as being picked up and given a bear hug. Differs from an ordinary tackle because of the hugger's feelings of love and need—and the huggee's feeling of warmth at being needed.

The ankle hug invariably says:

I am smaller than you are now, and I count on you.

Just touching you gives me security.

Back-to-front hug

Or waist-grabber.

A joyful gesture of support, especially for those engaged in routine household or humdrum chores.

A waist-grabber imparts the message:

Don't be so intent on getting the job done that you forget how much we mean to each other.

Friendship makes our workaday world go 'round.

Bear hug

Powerful. Secure. Use forbearance in making this hug firm rather than breathless.

A sampling of bear hug messages:

Let's both tap into the wonderful vitality we've been given.

I support you 100 percent.

Life is an adventure—and you're a big part of its newness and fun.

Cheek hug

Tender. Tasteful. Lightly given, it often has a spiritual quality.

A cheek hug can say:

I recognize that you are feeling fragile.

I care about you.

May my genuine concern for you give you strength.

Custom-tailored hug

A creative, special-order hug. Takes into account setting, situation, principals, and what is needed from the hug. Sometimes, to please a particular hugger, a favorite pet or toy is included. A custom-tailored hug can say almost anything you like.

I recognize that Gladys is very important to you and is jealous of our relationship. Let's include her in our hug.

Rumbles is important too, but he remains aloof. Maybe someday he will let down his guard and be part of our hug.

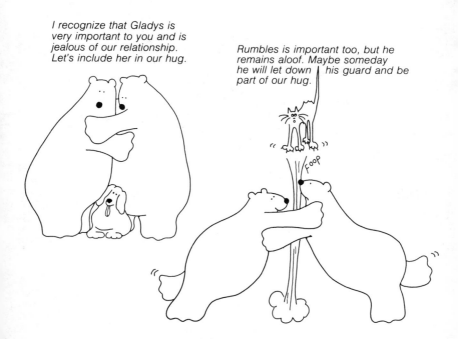

Grabber-squeezer hug

Playful, affectionate, brief. Offers the opportunity to work in a lot of fast hugging on a tight schedule. May be accompanied by a feeling of surprise.

A grabber-squeezer almost always says:

HoHO! Let's never grow too old to play.

Even when responsibilities keep us hopping, fun is an essential part of our lives.

I'm in a terrible hurry, but this is a quick reminder that I really like you.

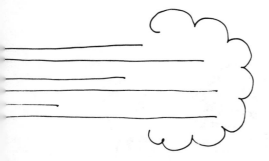

roup hug

Popular for good friends or associates. Combines well with team sports or singing in parts.

A group hug tells everybody in it:

We're all in this together.

One for all, and all for one.

Let's all share in the good feelings.

'Guess who?' hug

A frolicsome hug for longtime friends. Makes a gentle game out of an ordinary "hello" or "good day" greeting.

A "guess who?" hug has this to say:

If you guess who I am, I'll be happy you've thought about me. If you don't—well, mystery is part of the fun too.

We mustn't overlook the fact that humor is absolutely necessary for our well-being.

Heart-centered hug

Undistracted and unhurried. Perhaps the highest form of hugging. Acknowledges that place at the center of each of us where pure, unconditional love may be found.

A heart-centered hug says:

Feel our oneness as our bond of friendship grows.

I may frown on your naughtiness or misbehavior, but I don't love you any less.

Let's forgive each other—grudges are uncomfortable.

Sandwich hug

A three-way hug. Especially secure for the one in the middle.

Some messages of a sandwich hug:

Let's affirm our deep feeling of family closeness.

We're all equal shareholders in this friendship.

Let's make sure none of us is ever left out.

Side-to-side hug

Also known as a lateral squeeze. A merry, playful aside. Use it while strolling together or waiting in line.

Listen to what a side-to-side hug has to say:

Waiting around for gates to open is not a bit tedious because you're with me.

Being with you makes me feel good—wherever we are.

Top-of-the-head hug

Or cranial clasp.

Firm, supportive, strength-giving. Usually offered to a
seated huggee by a standing hugger. A gift of power
to one who is feeling stunned or frail or depressed.

The cranial clasp gives a clear message of strength:

*Tap into my positive energy if you are feeling
helpless today.*

*I'm ready to share my strength with you for as long
as you need it.*

ariations

Of course each basic hug type has numerous variations. If you are well-versed in these types and what each can say, you can augment your hug-message vocabulary limitlessly.

I'm here, Melissa.

Let's do hugs.

Scuba dooby doo.

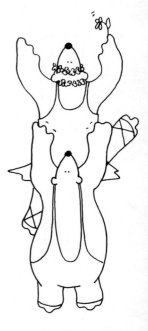

Pas de deux.

You're really handy, Harriet.

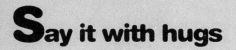

Say it with hugs

As your hugging vocabulary grows, you will find that the wonderful language of hugs is perfectly adapted to conveying everyday messages, especially in the areas of communication which follow.

Safety

Security

Trust

A HUG SAYS SAFETY

Regardless of our age or status in life, we all need to feel safe. When we do not feel safe, our actions may become inefficient, our interactions with others may lose their pleasure.

A hug creates a warm circle of support so that we can return to our tasks with a renewed sense of safety.

A hug says, *In my arms is a place where you can feel safe.*

A hug-for-safety statement is needed:

when stepping up to a podium to give a talk
   a hug says, *No need for accordion knees—just imagine everyone in the audience giving you a safe hug.*

when graduating—from anywhere
   a hug says, *You will find safe places in your new life too.*

when the night is full of shifting shadows
   a hug says, *Daylight will show you that shadows are really the safe shapes of ordinary things.*

Try a heart-centered hug to shut out fears and pass along a message of safeness.

You are safe here. Morning will come soon.

A hug keeps back the shadows.

A HUG SAYS SECURITY

Everyone needs to feel secure, but especially those on both ends of the age spectrum who depend on the love and good will of those who care for them.

A hug-for-security statement is needed:

by the very youngest trying out steps for the first time a hug says, *When the world you set out to explore seems frightening and complex, you can return any time to the security of my arms until you are ready to go out again and discover more.*

by the oldest trying out steps for the first time after
recovering from a fall

a hug says, *I will not allow you to become your
infirmity or lose your specialness or dignity or your
importance to me.*

Try a side-to-side or cheek hug to say security.

A HUG SAYS TRUST

Trust comes from the sense of security and safety we receive from others. Trust can free us to move when fear overwhelms our desire to participate in the exciting challenges of life.

Give a learn-to-trust hug message to:

a youth who needs reassurance that he is not alone in the difficult task of facing new responsibilities

    a hug says, *You do not have to do more or go faster or higher until you are ready. You can trust me to be here and support you through your journey into the adult world.*

a friend beginning a new venture in a new location with new associates

    a hug says, *Please take with you the feelings of trust you have learned here. I will continue to be your friend wherever you are.*

Sometimes a quick side-to-side hug is enough to reinforce a message of trust.

If you start to tip over, I'll be here.

You can trust us.

I trust you.

Self-worth
Belonging

A HUG SAYS SELF-WORTH

Self-worth is the foundation for satisfaction and success in our lives. This sense of personal value is created from the moment of birth, mostly by the messages others give us about ourselves.

Because the validation passed from generation to generation is often incomplete, many of us did not learn about our full worth when we were young. Now we have the chance to continue the process of affirmation, by giving the message through our hugs that we recognize the excellence of each individual.

A hug proclaims the innate worth of anyone:

a runner who does not quite qualify for a marathon,
an actress who muffs her lines,
a chef whose souffle flattens,
a batter who swings hard, but strikes out
   a hug says, *Self-worth and success are not synonyms. Trying is valuable. Being is valuable. Above all, YOU are valuable.*

one who has grown up with an uncomfortable sense of inadequacy, or even shame
   a hug says, *I have a real respect and affection for you. Please let me help you change your negative perceptions about yourself.*

Try a bear hug to pass along self-worth. (If the one you wish to hug is shy or fears intimacy, a gentler hug—like a cheek hug or a cranial clasp—may be more appropriate.)

You are wonderful, worthy, noble, kind, and interesting.

Also huggable.

A HUG SAYS BELONGING

Our sense of worth expands when we feel we belong—
first to intimate groups of relatives and friends, then to
the amazing family of living creatures everywhere.

When we feel our place within the embrace of this
universal connection, our hugs invite others into the
circle of life.

When "I" becomes "we," a hug speaks ardently of the
warmth of belonging:

for anyone who is part of a group sharing an ideal, a
project, a common interest, a game, a trade or
profession—or who is lucky enough just to have a
bunch of good friends

a hug says, *Your separateness and my separateness
add something unique and wonderful to this team
we're part of.*

This fellowship gives my life meaning.

A group hug can be the greatest voice of all for
self-worth and belonging.

Strength
Healing

A HUG SAYS STRENGTH

We often think of strength as a solitary energy that develops out of an individual's determination and toughness and self-responsibility. Of course responsibility-for-self is essential for personal power. But we can still pass along our inner vitality as a gift to others—to confirm and sustain their own strength and power.

Strength, particularly, is communicated as a bodily message. Touching and hugging are energizing. The wonder is: when we seek to transfer our energy in a hug, our own strength increases!

Sometimes you lean on me.

Give a gift-of-strength hug:

to someone left alone when a relationship dissolves
   a hug says, *When your faith in others has been
   damaged, let me hold you and fill you with strength.*

to a child feeling confused after a parent has moved
away from home
   a hug says, *You are not responsible for your
   parents' happiness. You have good friends in the
   world outside—and I'm one of them.*

to a not-so-young athlete, retiring from the game
   a hug says, *There are other strengths besides
   physical prowess. I honor what you have achieved.
   But most of all I really like who you are and who you
   will be.*

A heart-centered or bear hug is a
strength-giving statement.

Sometimes I lean on you.

A HUG SAYS HEALING

Our strength becomes a powerful healing force when given through physical contact. We have heard many-times-told stories of healing through touch. Now scientific research continues to confirm that touching and holding impart a life energy that heals—as well as supports and comforts—those suffering from illness or disease. New studies show that, to be truly therapeutic, touching must be coupled with an intent to help and to heal. Casual, offhand touching is less effective.

The vitality we receive from a therapeutic embrace contains this healing message: *I am alive and whole and I am coming home to my self.*

Give a healing hug to:

anyone who is trying to shake off an illness or infection or a bout with the blues, or whose broken body or spirit is mending

a hug says, *I will hold you so that you can draw strength from my support while you heal.*

My strength combined with yours is more than the sum of both our strengths. Feel that remarkable energy flowing into making you whole again!

A top-of-the-head hug speaks respectfully about healing.

Though I have confidence in my own skill, I also respect the miracle of your self-healing. I recognize a healing force that is more powerful than either of us.

Rx:

Four hugs a day for survival

Eight hugs a day for maintenance

Twelve hugs a day for growth

Appreciation

Happiness

Celebration

A HUG SAYS APPRECIATION

Appreciation for others and gratitude for the abundance and variety of life—these are flavors of happiness we communicate in an embrace.

When we are filled with thankfulness and appreciation, our hugs proclaim, *I'm grateful today for the deliciousness of life. Let's be sure to take the time to taste the richness of each moment.*

Let a hug voice your appreciation for:

a favorite teacher
   a hug says, *Thank you for making learning a never-ending adventure for me.*

a benefactor or a sponsor
   a hug says, *I am grateful for the miracles you help bring about in my life.*

one who offers you a new contract or career
   a hug says, *Thanks for the fresh challenge—and for your faith in me.*

a parent (now that you're grown up)
   a hug says, *What a great experience to know you now as an adult friend!*

someone whose words have inspired you
   a hug says, *Your messages have brought me
   serenity and helped me grow spiritually.*

a comic or jester
   a hug says, *Thanks for your cleverness and creative
   clowning. You make us whole as you make us laugh.*

An appreciative hug can be any kind—from a
side-to-side to a waist-grabber—depending on the
degree of closeness you feel toward the huggee.

I appreciate your humor.

Hug a clown.

A HUG SAYS HAPPINESS

Wonder, excitement, humor, contentment, and serenity are some of the shades of happiness that color our lives. When we live under a rainbow of these good feelings, our hearts overflow with an abundance of joy—so much joy that we have trouble NOT sharing it!

It's a delight to communicate our pleasure with a hug that says, *What a great day! I'm feeling so alive and wonderful! I'm overjoyed to share the excitement of this moment with you!*

Pass on the exhilarating lyrics of a happiness hug to:

your cohort in the discovery of a new idea
   a hug says, *What's more exciting than exchanging thoughts and finding an entirely new concept that makes life's pieces fit together!*

your golf or tennis partner

a hug says, *It's really a kick—just to be here with you, moving freely and laughing over the crazy things that happen in a game.*

a new friend beside you in a beautiful place—a lakeside, a hilltop, a street at festival time

a hug says, Wow! *What a view! What a place! I'm excited that you can see it with me.*

A quick back-to-front hug or grabber-squeezer heralds your happiness.

A HUG SAYS CELEBRATION

Celebration often means joining with others to share in the delight of a memorable event. We applaud and sing and feast and dance and laugh and cry at rituals that give meaning to our lives.

On these occasions we really need the language of hugs. A warm embrace is the happiest reward for a special moment, and says, *I am honored to be with you and to take part in these festivities.*

A back-to-front hug or bear hug, sandwich or group hug, custom-tailored or side-to-side hug—in fact, any kind of hug at all—sings out, *Let's celebrate!*

Yes!

But we don't have to wait for a special occasion to celebrate. We can celebrate who we are any time— here, now, sharing this world of marvels and miracles with those we care about.

We celebrate, too, our wonderful ability to communicate with hugs.

The language of hugs helps us speak from our hearts.

The language of hugs helps us see our true selves.

You are not really a bear.

You are not a bear either.

That extra touch

All of us need not only hugs, but other kinds of respectful touching as well. For some, hugging may even be uncomfortable. It may cause feelings of distress or fear because of cultural conditioning, physical trauma, or emotional deprivation. Sometimes just gently holding a hand, or giving a validating pat on the back, a playful head rub, a relaxing neck massage, or a kind touch on the arm may be a more sensitive way to communicate support.

Remember, although touching and hugging are of extraordinary value, the most cherished gift we can give is our acceptance of others' unique feelings and needs. This means that our decision to communicate through hugs or touch must always be based on respect for what is comfortable for that person.

Institute of Hug Therapy

We believe more must be done to break down the cultural and emotional barriers that prevent us from experiencing the healthy nourishment of touching and hugging. The establishment of the Institute of Hug Therapy is our whimsical, but earnest, contribution to that effort.

Become a member of the Institute of Hug Therapy by believing in the power of hugging and by following the ethics as set forth in *The Hug Therapy Book* and *Hug Therapy 2.*

Our hope is that hugging will become commonplace without detracting from the specialness of each hug.

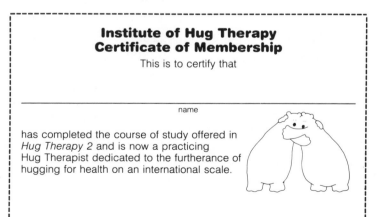

Institute of Hug Therapy
Certificate of Membership

This is to certify that

_____
name

has completed the course of study offered in
Hug Therapy 2 and is now a practicing
Hug Therapist dedicated to the furtherance of
hugging for health on an international scale.

About the author

Kathleen Keating Schloessinger, R. N., M. A., is author of the beloved little best seller, *The Hug Therapy Book,* now with over 500,000 sold in the United States alone. She is a psychiatric and mental health counselor, educator, and consultant. She conducts seminars and workshops internationally on the power of touch, as well as on stress management, parent education, communication and problem-solving skills, and group dynamics. Her experience also includes biofeedback research and consulting and administration in therapeutic communities. A former director of inservice education for Woodview-Calabasas Hospital in Calabasas, California, she has participated in many special seminars on a breadth of topics including Gestalt therapy.

She and her husband, Fred Schloessinger, now live in Toronto, Ontario, Canada.

The theme of her life is, she says, "to feel, know, and teach the many dimensions of love: the courage to struggle, the vulnerability to give and receive, the sensitivity to suffering, the power of anger, the openness to the delight of play, and the deep, deep pleasure of a warm embrace."

About the artist

Mimi Noland, designer of the gentle hug bears which appear in *The Hug Therapy Book, Hug Therapy 2, The Hug Therapy Book of Birthdays and Anniversaries,* and *The Love Therapy Book,* is a 1982 graduate of Skidmore College with a major in psychology. She is a writer and singer, a horse breeder and trainer, and has completed training to become a licensed police officer. She is the author of a nationally known book, *I Never Saw the Sun Rise,* written at the age of fifteen under the pen name of Joan Donlan. She lives near Minneapolis, Minnesota, on a farm with a houseful—and a barnful-—of animals.

Resources

Colton, Helen, *The Gift of Touch*. New York: Putnam, 1983. (Available from Family Forum, 1539 N. Courtney, Los Angeles, CA 90046.)

Keating, Kathleen. *The Hug Therapy Book* Minneapolis: CompCare Publishers, 1983.

Krieger, Delores. *Therapeutic Touch*. Englewood Cliffs, N.J.: Prentice-Hall, l979.

Lynch, James. *The Broken Heart.* New York: Basic Books, 1977.

Montagu, Ashley. *Touching: The Human Significance of the Skin.* New York: Columbia University Press, 1971.

Morris, Desmond. *Intimate Behavior.* New York: Bantam Books, 1973.

Simon, Sidney B. *Caring, Feeling, Touching.* Niles, Ill.: Argus Communications, 1976.

A Touch of Sensitivity, 50-minute video film produced by BBC Films, 1213 Wilmette Ave., Wilmette, IL 60091

The Touch Film with Dr. Jessie Potter, 22-minute film/video, Sterling Productions, 500 N. Dearborn St., No. 916, Chicago, IL 60610.

Name: _____
Diagnosis: Touch deprivation
Treatment Plan: An abundance of hugs
Prognosis: Excellent

HAZELDEN TITLES OF INTEREST:

Codependent No More: How to Stop Controlling Others and Start Caring for Yourself by Melody Beattie, $12.00
ISBN 0-89486-402-5   Order #5014

Boundaries: Where You End and I Begin
by Anne Katherine, M.A., $9.95
ISBN 1-56838-030-5   Order #7803

Finding Your Own Spiritual Path: An Everyday Guidebook by Peg Thompson, Ph.D., $12.00
ISBN 0-89486-912-4   Order #1509

Dancing Backwards in High Heels: How Women Master the Art of Resilience by Patricia O'Gorman, $12.00
ISBN 0-89486-998-1   Order #1494

A Woman's Spirit: More Meditations for Women by the author of *Each Day a New Beginning,* $10.00
ISBN 0-89486-869-1   Order #5433

Embodying Spirit: Coming Alive with Meaning and Purpose by Jacquelyn Small, $12.00
ISBN 0-89846-994-9   Order #1489

The Little Book of Joy: An Interactive Journal for Thoughts, Prayers, and Wishes, by Bill Zimmerman with illustrations by Tom Bloom, $8.95
ISBN 1-56838-041-0   Order #1314

Call to Purpose: How Men Make Sense of Life Changing Experiences by Richard Solly, $11.95
ISBN 1-56838-045-3   Order #1312

To receive a free catalog of Hazelden books and merchandise, or to place an order, call toll-free:
800-328-0098

All titles are also available at your local bookstore.

For information on Hazelden's treatment programs and facilities, call toll-free: 800-257-7800

HAZELDEN